THE LIBRARY OF HIP-HOP BIOGRAPHIES™

Sean Combs

Philip Wolny

Slade Media Center

92
P DIDDY

3SLAD00065374E

The Rosen Publishing Group, Inc.
New York

Published in 2006 by The Rosen Publishing Group, Inc.
29 East 21st Street, New York, NY 10010

Library of Congress Cataloging-in-Publication Data

Wolny, Philip.
Sean Combs/by Philip Wolny.—1st ed.
    p. cm.—(The library of hip-hop biographies)
Includes bibliographical references and index.
ISBN 1-4042-0516-0 (library binding)
1. P. Diddy, 1970– —Juvenile literature. 2. Rap musicians—United States—Biography—Juvenile literature. I. Title. II. Series.

ML3930.P84W65 2006
782.421649'092—dc22

                                                2005021325

Manufactured in the United States of America

On the cover: Sean Combs performs at the 2005 MTV Video Music Awards at the American Airlines Arena in Miami, Florida, on August 28, 2005.

CONTENTS

INTRODUCTION

Sean "Diddy" Combs has traveled a long way to the top of the world. When you hear the words "ghetto fabulous," "benjamins," and "bad boy," the first name that comes to mind is probably Diddy. Combs, who is also known as Puffy, Puff, Puff Daddy, and P. Diddy has had as many ups and downs as he has had name changes.

From humble, middle-class beginnings, Combs has skyrocketed to incredible heights of wealth and fame. The songs he created or had a hand in making have sold tens of millions of copies. His company, Bad Boy Entertainment, has changed the rules for fashion and music. Along the way, he has brought hip-hop to millions of new listeners and has given a new twist to what it is to be an entrepreneur in America.

His influence has touched millions, and it is the product of hard work. There has been as much tragedy as triumph on his way to the top. He has seen the loss of close friends and has risked everything to keep Bad Boy on the map. All the while, he has never stopped working and giving back to those who look up to him. As he claims in one of his biggest hits, "Can't nobody hold P. Diddy down." This is the story of Sean "Diddy" Combs, the self-described "bad boy for life."

CHAPTER ONE

GETTING IN THE GAME

Sean Combs was born in Harlem in New York City on November 4, 1970. Though Harlem was mostly a neglected ghetto at this time, the Combs family lived in a relatively nice area and enjoyed a more or less middle-class existence.

Tragedy struck the Combs family early in Sean's life, however. His father, Melvin, a streetwise hustler and drug dealer, was shot to death near Central Park when Sean was only three years old. His mother, Janice, a former model, worked many jobs at once to keep the family afloat. Eventually, in 1982, they moved to the New York suburb of Mount Vernon, a working-class area just north of the Bronx.

Sean Combs inherited his mother's work ethic. At age twelve he had two paper routes (one applied for secretly under his friend's name) and worked other jobs as well, including one at an amusement park. He didn't care that some of the kids made fun of him for always working. He knew that hard work would take him where we wanted to go in life.

Though he had moved, Combs stayed in touch with his Harlem roots and old friends there. He attended an after-school program in Harlem every day. It was in his old neighborhood that, as a teenager, he found his true calling in life: hip-hop. This was the era when Run-D.M.C. and LL Cool J were starting to put hip-hop on the map. An excellent, show-stopping dancer, Combs would sneak out to the clubs late at night because he couldn't get enough of the scene. By the time of his high school graduation, he had danced in music videos for artists such as rapper Doug E. Fresh and pop group Fine Young Cannibals. He dreamed of being a success and felt his love of hip-hop was a way to get there.

It was as a teenager, too, that he gained the nickname Puffy. According to Ronin Ro's biography on Combs, *Bad Boy*, Combs would sometimes lose his temper and "puff up." The nickname stuck, and he eventually embraced it.

Sean Combs dances on stage during a concert at the Point Theatre in Dublin, Ireland, on March 14, 2000. Dance has always been a large part of the rapper's reputation. As a teenager, he won praise in nightclubs for his fancy dance moves. Despite his tremendous success as an entertainer and business executive, he remains a party boy at heart.

LIFE OF THE PARTY

In 1988, Combs started attending Howard University, a prestigious historically black university in Washington, D.C. It was there that he discovered he had a knack for throwing hip-hop parties, which soon made him a campus legend. While exploring many other moneymaking schemes, he soon realized that parties were a way to make money and to network with hip-hop stars and other movers and shakers. He made special efforts to meet popular rappers, artists, and businesspeople associated with hip-hop.

GOING UPTOWN

Combs's first big breakthrough came when he landed a coveted internship at Uptown Records in New York. Former rapper Andre Harrell had started Uptown and built it into a successful company. His first big hit had been with Heavy D, a young rapper who had also grown up in Mount Vernon. Heavy D made accessible, crossover hip-hop dubbed new jack swing. This hip-hop had a cleaner image than much of the more streetwise acts making it big in the late 1980s.

New jack swing fit Harrell's vision of the "ghetto fabulous" movement. This was a movement that recognizes hip-hop's middle-class center. It highlights artists in flashy suits rhyming about love and success rather than the gritty reality of the streets. It became the model for a young Combs to emulate and improve on later, with incredible results.

Combs commuted from Howard University four hours each way twice a week while interning at Uptown. He dived into his work at Uptown. He learned everything he could from everyone he got in touch with. Harrell soon recognized that Combs was the hardest-working intern he had ever seen.

Combs's first real breakthrough was with the newcomers Jodeci, who arrived at Uptown from North Carolina with twenty-two songs on a mix tape. Puffy set to work on distinguishing

Andre Harrell *(left)* founded Uptown Records in 1987, after spending several years as a music executive at Def Jam Records. Heavy D *(right)* was one of the first artists whom he signed to the label and the prototype of the smoother, soulful hip-hop sound that became Uptown's signature. They are pictured here at a celebrity birthday party in Los Angeles, California, on June 26, 2005.

Jodeci from the rest of an already crowded rhythm and blues (R & B) scene. He did so by remaking Jodeci to dress more like the everyday fans he saw at clubs and on the street: sports jerseys, baggy pants, baseball caps, jewelry, and cell phones, which were luxurious items at the time.

Harrell was so impressed with Combs that he soon promoted Combs from intern to vice president of artists and repertoire (A and R). A and R executives are often the ones at record companies to scout, sign, and develop new talent. For such a young man, this was an impressive move. Puffy also guided his artists in the studio—he bragged to coworkers that he had "platinum ears."

THE CITY COLLEGE TRAGEDY

Combs continued to promote parties and other events as he distinguished himself at Uptown. In December 1991, he and Heavy D decided to throw a charity basketball event at City College of New York (CCNY) in uptown Manhattan. The event was intended to raise money for the fight against AIDS.

Early on, everything started to go seriously wrong. A huge line had formed outside the CCNY gymnasium hours before the event. The crowd grew anxious and unruly while waiting. People tried to push their way into the venue but were obstructed by locked doors. When the dust had cleared, eight people had been crushed to death.

Major news outlets attacked Combs, Heavy D, and the other organizers for their perceived lack of preparation. It took years for the courts to apportion blame for the tragedy. An official report of the deputy mayor's office, while admonishing Combs and Heavy D, also blamed CCNY, the police, and even emergency medical services workers, who were seen as slow to respond.

Combs was traumatized by the event and racked with guilt. He said that his faith in God was the only thing that helped him get through this terrible time.

CHAPTER TWO

MAKING IT "BIG"

In 1992, Sean "Puffy" Combs was ready to make bigger moves at Uptown. His next major break-through would be his work with seventeen-year-old Mary J. Blige from Yonkers, New York. It was Combs who urged his mentor to sign her as fast as possible. Blige had grown up in the hip-hop era and her fusion of soul music with hip-hop beats reflected this. This was the "ghetto fabulous" sound that Combs and Harrell were looking for. Combs saw it as the next, unstoppable wave of chart-topping music.

To ease her into the public eye, Combs had hip-hop artists make guest appearances on songs he was working on with Blige. "Real Love," the first single off her first album, *What's the 411?*, went to number seven on the pop charts. Combs had found another winner on his own way to the top.

STRIKING OUT ON HIS OWN

Despite his success, or per-haps because of it, Combs felt he had outgrown Uptown Records. For years, even as a young boy, he had yearned

Mary J. Blige's debut album *What's the 411?* was an instant smash. Within a year after its release, critics were calling her the queen of hip-hop soul, a nickname that has stuck.

to start his own company. In recent years, he had envisioned starting a record company called Bad Boy, patterned after Uptown but even more ambitious.

Andre Harrell helped Puffy to realize his dream. The new company, which would be a part of Uptown, would handle management, recording, and production for Combs's own clients.

Around the same time, a DJ named Mister Cee gave a demo of an unknown young rapper named Christopher Wallace, also known as Biggie Smalls, to Combs. When Combs heard the demo, he knew immediately that he had something special.

He sought out Wallace, a poor kid from Brooklyn's rough Bedford Stuyvesant neighborhood. Wallace, once a talented student, had dropped out of high school and was selling drugs and guns. His greatest talent, though, was as a lyricist with a commanding, incredible flow (the way a rapper says his words over a beat). Over lunch, Combs hooked the young rapper with his enthusiasm. Wallace agreed verbally to sign with Uptown. It was the start of a relationship that would lead to unimaginable success for both men—and also unbearable tragedy.

NOTORIOUS

Combs was excited—the sound he and Wallace were making combined hard-core appeal for the streets with the smoothness and discipline Puffy enjoyed in R & B. It was a rougher version of the ghetto fabulous sound he was trying to make into a movement, but it fit in nonetheless.

Combs (right) and Chris "Notorious B.I.G." Wallace pose for the cameras at the MTV Video Music Awards in New York City in September 1995. By this time, Notorious B.I.G.'s debut album was wildly successful, confirming Combs's reputation of having a knack for recruiting appealing hip-hop talent.

SELECTED DISCOGRAPHY

Jodeci, *Forever My Lady*, 1991 (MCA/Uptown Records)

Mary J. Blige, *What's the 411?*, 1992 (MCA/Uptown Records)

Craig Mack, *Project: Funk da World*, 1994 (Bad Boy)

Faith Evans, *Faith*, 1995 (Bad Boy)

Notorious B.I.G., *Ready to Die*, 1994 (Bad Boy)

112, *112*, 1996 (Bad Boy)

Notorious B.I.G., *Life After Death*, 1997 (Bad Boy)

Puff Daddy and the Family, *No Way Out*, 1997 (Bad Boy)

Ma$e, *Harlem World*, 1997 (Bad Boy)

Ma$e, *Double Up*, 1999 (Bad Boy)

Puff Daddy, *Forever*, 1999 (Bad Boy)

Notorious B.I.G., *Born Again*, 1999 (Bad Boy)

Black Rob, *Life Story*, 1999 (Bad Boy)

Dream, *It Was All a Dream*, 2001 (Bad Boy)

P. Diddy and the Bad Boy Family, *The Saga Continues*, 2001 (Bad Boy)

Various Artists, *P. Diddy and Bad Boy Records Present: We Invented the Remix*, 2002 (Bad Boy)

Various Artists, *Bad Boys II* [Soundtrack], 2003, (Bad Boy)

By this time, Puffy had convinced Wallace to change his stage name from Biggie Smalls (already being used by another artist) to the Notorious B.I.G., though most friends and foes still called him Biggie. He later told journalists that the acronym stood for "Business Instead of Game."

A SERIOUS SETBACK

This initial success was not without controversy, however. Uptown's parent company, MCA Records, thought Biggie's lyrics were too hardcore. Harrell took MCA's side. He thought that Biggie, while potentially profitable, did not fit Uptown's middle-class, good-times image. Some observers also speculated that Harrell resented his protégé's success. Whatever the case, in July 1993, Harrell invited Combs into his office and fired him.

Janice Combs has been a visible figure in her son's career, and is herself a minor celebrity. Combs has put a number of business ventures in her name, including a music publishing company and a talent management company.

Combs was shocked and heartbroken. He felt that Harrell had been like the father he had never known. Up until that moment, he had also been living in Harrell's plush New Jersey home. Combs was evicted from there as well as the Uptown offices. Though it was a major stumbling block, it turned out to be just the thing to push Combs out on his own and into superstardom.

PICKING HIMSELF UP AGAIN

After a few days of shock and recovery, Combs went right back to work making his dreams a reality. He moved Bad Boy into Janice Combs's Westchester home and hired a few old Howard classmates to help run the company. They worked fifteen-hour days, sharing one computer among them. Combs demanded that everyone start work promptly at 8 AM every day and give him detailed progress reports at the end of every workday.

Meanwhile, Combs had to convince Biggie, also released from Uptown, that he should stick to making music. Biggie had not seen much money so far from his music and realized that he made far more money dealing drugs. He vowed to return to dealing if their fortunes did not change soon.

Fortune soon smiled on Combs. The buzz around him in the industry was very positive. He forged on with Bad Boy and met with prospective investors. Clive Davis, a legendary music executive known for his ability to pick hits, met with Combs on behalf of Arista Records. Soon, he inked Combs to a $15 million distribution deal.

Armed with this sudden influx of cash, Combs tracked down Biggie, who had fallen in with a rough crowd in North Carolina. He told Biggie to return to New York as soon as possible; he would have a contract and a check waiting for him the next day. Biggie did just that.

CHAPTER THREE

TRAGEDY AND TRIUMPH

The newly revived Bad Boy's first release was "Flava in Ya Ear," by Brentwood, Long Island, native Craig Mack. The success of the single, which went platinum, would catapult Mack's full-length *Project: Funk da World*, released in 1994, to gold-record status.

That year, Sean "Puffy" Combs also had high hopes for the talented Faith Evans, who had sung backup vocals on recordings for various R & B artists, including Mary J. Blige. Shortly after she signed with Bad Boy, Evans began dating Biggie. Within the span of a few weeks, they married.

With some help from Blige, Combs made another key addition to the Bad Boy roster with the signing of the Lox, a trio of rappers from Blige's hometown. As lyricists, songwriters, and guest stars, the Lox would be involved with many of Bad Boy's future hits.

BAD BOY BLOWS UP

The artist who would have the greatest staying power for Bad Boy, however, was the Notorious B.I.G. In the summer of 1994, Combs released Biggie's "Juicy/Unbelievable" single, which quickly went gold. It was part of a winning formula: releasing a radio-friendly song with a hard-core anthem on the B side of the tape.

In September 1994, Biggie's first full-length record, *Ready to Die*, came out. It became an instant classic, combining skillful rhyming, R & B–flavored grooves, and tales of the street life. The commercial and critical success of *Ready to Die* signaled that Bad Boy was poised to become a major presence in hip hop.

Combs continued to build on his label's success in 1995 and 1996. He released "Can't You See," the first single from Total, a female R & B trio. Faith Evans's record, *Faith*, came out in August 1995 and dazzled audiences with its soulful ballads.

Combs had also signed a four-man singing group he renamed 112 after the club where he met them to sign the contract. Its self-titled debut dropped in August 1996 and spawned two big hits, "Cupid" and "Only You." "Only You" was particularly notable because Combs took the opportunity to include a cameo from a brand-new Bad Boy artist: Ma$e.

Combs and Biggie perform at a concert in 1996. The two had developed a strong friendship in the few years that they had known each other, and their partnership as record executive and artist was quite fruitful. Combs's association with Biggie helped to raise Biggie's already imposing profile.

Ma$e (born Mason Betha) was a young rapper who became one of Combs's brightest stars. Originally calling himself Murder Ma$e, the Harlem native traveled down to Atlanta, Georgia. There, he received a standing ovation from the crowd while performing at a party. Combs decided to offer him a recording contract on the spot. The two quickly became a duo, and Combs took Ma$e under his wing.

Combs poses with Ma$e at the Billboard Music Awards on December 8, 1997, after winning awards for best rap artist and best rap single. The following year, Ma$e won the best rap artist award.

RECOGNITION

In addition to Bad Boy's tremendous record sales, Combs also received official recognition from the industry in June 1996. During the American Society of Composers, Artists and Publishers (ASCAP) Rhythm and Soul Music Awards, Biggie and Combs shared songwriting credits for top rap song of the year for "One More Chance/Stay with Me." Even more impressively, ASCAP named Combs songwriter of the year. Bad Boy singles had been high on the charts the whole year.

Commercially, the summer of 1996 was a good one for Combs and Bad Boy. Due to his smooth raps and good looks, Ma$e was becoming an MTV heartthrob. Also, 112 was becoming a staple with R & B audiences.

The East/West Beef

While Bad Boy was making big waves on the charts, other events — including a feud between Biggie and Tupac Shakur — would lead to trouble for its successful leader. The saga of Biggie and Tupac began when the two met on the set of Tupac's movie *Poetic Justice* in 1993. During the next two years, Tupac and Biggie would hang out a lot. Tupac even had Biggie open for him on tour when the latter was relatively unknown.

A year later, the relationship quickly deteriorated. The downward spiral began when Tupac was shot at a Manhattan recording studio during a robbery. Combs, Biggie, and other members of Bad Boy were in the same studio that night, and Tupac publicly accused them of being involved in the attack.

In the meantime, Tupac had served a jail sentence for an unrelated offense and had been bailed out by Marion "Suge" Knight, the owner of Death Row Records, based in Los Angeles.

FIRST BLOOD

The bad blood between the two camps worsened when Knight told an uneasy audience at the August 1995 Source Awards in New York, "If you don't want the owner of your label on your album or in your video, or on your tour, come to Death Row." Everyone knew he was taking a slap at Combs, who appeared in most of his artists' videos and on many of their tracks.

Combs later expressed shock to *Vibe*, saying, "I couldn't believe what he said . . . I thought we was boys." Much like Biggie and Tupac, Combs and Knight had been on friendly terms. In some ways, Combs had modeled his younger company on Death Row's example: both companies considered themselves part of a movement, with Death Row doing gangsta rap and Bad Boy bringing "ghetto fabulous" to the masses.

Soon after, members of both camps were at a birthday event in Atlanta, Georgia, when Knight's employee and longtime friend Jake Robles was gunned down in front of the club. Knight had rushed out of the club and was face to face with Combs when the shots rang out and killed his friend. Knight reportedly told Combs that he thought Combs had something to do with the shooting.

Again, Combs was astounded at the accusation and soon found himself countering similar claims from the media. Magazines like the *Source* and *Vibe* fueled the fire by writing sensational stories that connected Combs to the slaying.

Tension was running high between the two labels. The Bad Boy and Death Row entourages nearly rioted at the Tenth Annual Soul Train Awards in Los Angeles, the first time Tupac and Biggie ran into each other since Tupac was wounded. Luckily, nothing came of it that night.

On September 7, 1996, in Las Vegas, Nevada, Knight and Tupac were riding in an SUV. A car pulled up and an unknown gunman shot Tupac four times. Tupac died six days later. Biggie and Combs were also concerned because, once again, rumors linked them to the tragedy.

THE DARKEST HOUR

In the months after Tupac's death, Combs and Biggie continued working together and tried to withdraw from the tension of the

Tupac Shakur *(left)* made a forceful impression on the music industry in his short career, and is widely considered by hip-hop fans to be one of the greatest rappers of all time. A prolific artist, he spent considerable time in the studio, as evidenced by the numerous recordings that have been released since his death. The rapper, shown here with Marion "Suge" Knight at the Luxor Hotel in Las Vegas, Nevada, on November 1, 1995, was also a promising movie actor.

feud. They made appeals to the media in an effort to dispel the rumors swirling around. Biggie declared that he loved California and planned to eventually move his family there. He even recorded a new take on LL Cool J's 1988 classic "Goin' Back to Cali," which lauded the state.

Combs and Biggie traveled to California in February 1997 for a promotional tour and to record some new tracks. On March 9, 1997, they attended a party hosted by *Vibe* in

Thousands of mourners came out to pay last respects to the Notorious B.I.G. as his funeral procession made its way through the streets of Fort Greene, Brooklyn, on March 18, 1997.

Los Angeles. After the party, the Bad Boy entourage piled into a caravan of vehicles. They were stopped at a red light when gunshots riddled Biggie's vehicle.

Once the coast seemed clear, Combs rushed to his friend's aid and found the big man slumped over the passenger-side dashboard. Everyone sped off to the nearest hospital, and Combs prayed frantically for his friend's life. His prayers were in vain: thirty minutes later, Biggie was pronounced dead.

With everyone begging him to leave Los Angeles for his own safety, Combs took a plane back to New York the next day. He broke down in tears at the airport; he couldn't believe he was leaving without his friend.

"I'LL BE MISSING YOU"

Through the shock, horror, and grief, Combs put his faith in God once more. He realized that Biggie would have wanted him to

Sean Combs and Sting (the former lead singer of the Police) perform a medley of "I'll Be Watching You" and "I'll Be Missing You" at the MTV Video Music Awards at New York City's Radio City Music Hall on September 4, 1997.

continue the work they had done. Combs also wanted to honor the memory of his friend and most successful artist who had helped him build the Bad Boy empire.

One day, he saw the video for the Police's "I'll Be Watching You" on MTV. One of his favorite songs as a youngster, it inspired him to get back to work immediately. He recruited Faith Evans and 112 to do a tribute song for Biggie. He employed his trademark hands-on style in studio—he wanted to do it just right.

The new song, "I'll Be Missing You," was an instant success. It entered the Billboard Top 100 at number one and stayed there for eleven weeks, three weeks longer than the Police's original hit in 1984.

The song joined other Bad Boy triumphs that season. Combs had decided to release Biggie's second album as scheduled in March 1997, a month after Biggie's death. Eerily titled *Life After Death*, it spawned a slew of hit singles, including "Hypnotize" and "Mo Money, Mo Problems," which warned, ironically, of the perils of fame and success. The album stayed on the charts for almost two years and sold 10 million copies.

No Way Out

The tragedy of Biggie's death helped Combs focus on his next big project, which had actually been in the works for some time: a solo record by Puff Daddy, the artist and MC. The troubled CEO and producer had a lot on his mind: the loss of a friend, the promotion of his company and its music, and various other business ventures. At times, the pressure felt unbearable, but he kept going. He didn't know how to quit. He felt the need to express himself through music, and he hoped the record would help dispel some ghosts.

The record *No Way Out* was released on July 22, 1997, and quickly hit number one on the charts, selling half a million copies its first week. The singles "Can't Nobody Hold Me Down," "All About the Benjamins," and "Been Around the

World" were huge successes. Puff Daddy and the Family seemed to be on MTV and other stations around the clock.

Many people criticized Combs during this era, the greatest one for Bad Boy financially. Critics felt that he had capitalized on the death of Biggie to sell records. Others pointed out that the glossy image of his stars placed too much emphasis on materialism. They said his raps were too commercial and too bland, and that most of the samples were lifted entirely from older music. Many hard-core rap fans scoffed at Bad Boy's image—the shiny silver suits, the self-promotion, and Combs in every video, rapping on every song. They saw Bad Boy's artists as sellouts.

Despite strong criticism, Combs aggressively pushed the ghetto fabulous image throughout the late 1990s. From photographs on album covers to live performances, most representations of Bad Boy's artists showcased the label's over-the-top dress code.

Puffy countered that his main goal was to entertain people. He had no desire to be a gangster or to describe life on the ghetto streets, though some of Bad Boy's output touched upon those subjects. Instead, he saw himself giving the public what it wanted. He embraced white, suburban audiences along with the traditional hip-hop audience. He felt that Bad Boy's crossover hits brought people together.

Regarding his sampling of old hits, he felt he was making the hits of yesteryear fresh for a new audience. Many of those artists made more money in royalties from his songs than they ever did with the originals. It was a win-win situation for everyone involved, including the record-buying public.

A RISING STAR

In 1999, some members left the Bad Boy family. Combs said the departures were friendly ones. The Lox got out of its contract and signed with the Ruff Ryders label. Its debut record *Money, Power, Respect*, released in January 1998, had made it to number three on the charts. Plus, it had appeared on many Bad Boy singles or had cowritten them. However, the group wanted a more hard-core sound than Combs's crossover hip-hop.

A bigger surprise was the departure of Ma$e. Combs was shocked. Ma$e's second album, *Double Up*, was about to be released. But Ma$e had found religion and had tired of the life of a superstar. He later became a preacher and formed S.A.N.E. Ministries.

Puffy had high hopes for another talented newcomer. Jamaal "Shyne" Barrow had, like Biggie, grown up in Brooklyn for much of his childhood. Combs made an aggressive effort to sign Shyne. The trademark Bad Boy house sound had been highly profitable. But Combs recognized that a good part of the hip-hop audience yearned for more "authentic" performers. Shyne inspired comparisons to Biggie, with a smooth yet hard-core flow and low-pitched voice. In the end, Bad Boy signed Shyne for "at least $1 million," according to *Newsweek* magazine.

Combs and Shyne became inseparable, especially once Ma$e left the scene. Combs showed the young artist the good life, buying him fine jewelry, fancy cars, and taking him out on the town regularly. "That was when he was the Michael Jackson of hip-hop," Shyne later told the *Village Voice*. "I went every-where with him . . . Combs was one of the biggest people in the world, and I was just going along for that joyride."

THE CLUB NEW YORK TRAGEDY

Combs was soon seen about town with actress and singer Jennifer Lopez. They had been friends for a while before going out as a couple, and he had recorded several tracks for her hit record *On the 6* in 1998. The media could not get enough of the power couple. The two seemed like they were joined at the hip. According to E-Online, Combs was "absolutely smitten." But the relationship would fade after one of the most difficult times Combs ever had to go through.

Combs, his bodyguard Anthony "Wolf" Jones, Lopez, Shyne, and others were partying at Club New York on December 27, 1999. On their way out of the crowded dance club, they got into a scuffle with a man, and Shyne reportedly pulled a gun. Shots were fired, but it was never determined who fired first.

Shyne later claimed that he fired his gun into the air, in hopes of defending his mentor and friend. He then fled.

Combs, Lopez, and Jones also fled, but soon they were pulled over by the police, who arrested them after a gun was found in Combs's vehicle. Lopez was soon cleared of any wrongdoing and was released. However, Combs, Jones, and Shyne were not off the hook. The case would come to trial almost a year later, in the fall of 2000. Famed attorney Johnnie Cochran represented Combs and Jones, while Shyne had his own lawyer. Combs and Jones were charged with weapons possession and bribery—the prosecutor claimed that they tried to have the limo driver take the blame for the gun found in the car.

Combs was anxious. He professed his innocence at every opportunity. But he knew that the prosecutors were aiming for him. He felt that his fame had made him a target and worried that juries sometimes convicted the wrong person. Combs later told Sway Calloway of MTV News that the holiday season marked the worst of times for him during the trial. "It was a real dark time . . . where I was losing a lot of weight [from stress]." Combs and Lopez even split up from the stress of the charges and the negative publicity they both received.

In the end, Combs and his bodyguard were cleared of all charges. But it was a bittersweet victory. Shyne received a ten-year prison term, having been found guilty of weapons possession, assault, and reckless endangerment. After the verdict, Cochran pressured Shyne's family that Combs would do all he could for them during the appeals process.

This courtroom drawing shows Assistant District Attorney Matthew Bogdanos (*left, with gun*) presenting his final arguments to the jury during the trial of Sean Combs (*center*) on March 13, 2001. Others represented in the drawing are codefendants Anthony "Wolf" Jones (*right*), Jamaal "Shyne" Barrow (*second from right*), and State Supreme Court Justice Charles Solomon (*third from right*).

Combs now felt that he needed a change. The nicknames Puffy, Puff Daddy, and Puff were tainted, so he decided to reinvent himself again, this time with a new name. From that point on, he would be known as P. Diddy, a play on his old nickname.

CHAPTER FOUR

A MAN FOR ALL SEASONS

Sean "P. Diddy" Combs has never been one to put all his eggs into one basket. He has built his empire not just as a record company, but also as a collection of profitable businesses. These include Justin's, the restaurant chain he started in 1997; Blueflame, a marketing company; and various other side projects. In recent years, he's made his mark in a new frontier—as an actor, both in films and on the Broadway stage. At the same time, he has continued giving back to the community.

FASHION MAVEN

Combs started his clothing company, Sean John, in 1997. True to form, he named it after himself. He was inspired by one of his heroes, Russell Simmons, the cofounder of the hugely successful Def Jam Recordings who started his own clothing empire, Phat Farm, in 1992.

Like Simmons, Combs aimed to put out high-quality casual clothing for the hip-hop generation. Just as he popularized the ghetto fabulous lifestyle in his music and videos, he has worked to blend high fashion and hip-hop. This was not lim-

This is the flagship store of Combs's clothing line Sean John. It occupies a prime location on New York City's premiere retail destination, Fifth Avenue. In 2005, Sean John was the fastest-growing sportswear line for men.

ited to traditional, loose-fitting hip-hop gear. As Jeff Tweedy, who ran Sean John, told *USA Weekend* magazine, "People assumed that because Combs was a hip-hop star, it was just gonna be baggy pants and big shirts . . . But I could tell by our conversations he was serious about taking fashion in a new direction."

Sean John is now a major component of the Bad Boy empire. Sales rose from $30 million in 1999 to a staggering $450 in 2002. Sean John has also achieved critical success. From 2000 to 2003,

Combs celebrates winning the Menswear Designer of the Year award backstage at the CFDA Fashion Awards in New York City on June 7, 2004. With him is Zac Posen, another award winner.

the Council of Fashion Designers of America (CFDA) nominated Sean John for design excellence at its prestigious annual awards gala. In June 2004, Combs was named designer of the year by the CFDA.

MAKING DA BAND

Combs has always changed with the times and tried new things. When the reality television craze started catching on in 2002, he dived right in. MTV had great success with *Making the Band*, a show on which industry players form a band from scratch from among thousands of aspiring musicians. Combs put his own spin on it and signed on to star and coproduce *Making the Band 2*. This time, he would personally pick and choose a group of aspiring rap and R & B stars and groom them into a successful group he named Da Band.

It was a new way of trying to make hits for Combs. Real talent he said, such as Notorious B.I.G. or Mary J. Blige, lands on your doorstep when you least expect it, and it's hard to force the issue. Though it made for great television, tensions sometimes hit the boiling point. This was especially true when Combs had the young members of Da Band doing menial tasks, like trekking for miles from Manhattan to Junior's restaurant in Brooklyn to fetch him the restaurant's famous cheesecake. But the mogul wanted to see how dedicated they were to becoming stars. He knew that one needs to have a thick skin to make it to the top.

BAD BOY DOES GOOD

Combs is more than a hard-driving, demanding disciplinarian. He is also a successful artist who gives something back to society. For years, he has put his vast riches and tremendous amounts of time into helping people, especially underprivileged youth.

In 1995, he founded Daddy's House Social Programs, Inc., a nonprofit company financed by himself, Bad Boy, and other donors. Daddy's House concentrates on education for inner-city youth, sponsoring such activities as after-school programs, trips for high-school seniors scouting colleges, and summer camps. It gives youngsters jobs and internships with the various Bad Boy companies. From donating computers to New York City schools to throwing a Thanksgiving dinner for 30,000 of Atlanta's homeless and poor, the only thing bigger than Combs's wallet is his heart.

STAR OF STAGE AND SCREEN

Combs had been a producer, executive, restaurateur, clothing manufacturer, and philanthropist. It probably came as no surprise

GOING THE EXTRA MILE

In the summer of 2003, Combs decided to go the extra mile for the kids, quite literally. He announced, on short notice, that he would run the New York City Marathon. It would be for charity, and he would be accepting donations, all going to the underfunded New York City school system. In the weeks before, Combs went on a media blitz to publicize the cause and even had a reality show about his training aired on MTV.

It was not easy, however. According to the *New York Times*, most runners train for months, and Combs only had eight weeks. Worse, he suffered a knee injury while training that bothered him for weeks. It flared up again during the race itself, and his legs nearly cramped up after 12 miles (19.3 kilometers). But the same drive that put him on top of the world got him to the finish line. For an inexperienced runner, completing a 26.2-mile (42.2 km) marathon in four hours and fourteen minutes was impressive. More important, he raised $2 million for New York City schoolchildren, $1 million more than expected.

to his fans that their hero would try his hand at acting next. Combs's first onscreen appearance was in 2001, in the mob-themed comedy/drama *Made*. He played Ruiz, an underworld figure who grills two bumbling Mafia errand boys visiting New York. Later that year, he undertook a more dramatic role in *Monster's Ball*, in which he played Halle Berry's character's husband, who is condemned to death row.

Sean Combs runs the final stretch of the New York City Marathon on November 2, 2003. By enlisting corporate sponsors such as Nike, MTV, McDonald's, Footlocker, and his own Sean John, as well as a host of other celebrities, he raised more than $2 million to support public education in the city.

Perhaps his most grueling test as an actor, however, was on Broadway. Many people were surprised (and some rather critical) when Combs was picked to play a major role in the stage classic *A Raisin in the Sun*, opposite Phylicia Rashad. But Combs impressed even the skeptics by putting in able performances when the play opened in April 2004.

THE NEXT FRONTIER

For Sean Combs, there is always more work to be done. Whether it's in music, fashion, the restaurant business, or acting, he is always looking for the next challenge.

In 1999, Bad Boy released Black Rob's full-length record, *Life Story*, to critical and commercial success. Supported by its popular single, "Whoa!," the album hit number three on the Billboard Top 100. That year, Combs signed Dream, a female vocal group. It represented a change for him, since Dream was the first teen pop group on Bad Boy. The group's 2001 album, *It Was All a Dream*, also scored big on the charts.

Bad Boy also had success with traditional R & B acts such as Carl Thomas and Mario Winans. Combs has continued putting out hip-hop, too, and he has high hopes for a slew of recent signings, including Queens, New York, rapper Aasim and veteran Southern rappers Eightball and MJG. Ma$e returned to Bad Boy and released a comeback album, *Welcome Back*, where he mixed his usual boasts with moral lessons. Compilation albums such as the soundtrack to the film *Bad Boys II* also proved to be big hits. The 2002 album *We Invented the Remix* was a proud return to form for the label that went multiplatinum. Combs's new solo record, entitled *S. Combs,* is in the works for the fall of 2005. It will bear his new nickname, Diddy, as he officially dropped the "P."

Combs has branched out into all facets of broadcast media. In addition to working on *Making the Band 3*, in which he grooms a new female vocal group for MTV, he has parlayed his long relationship with the network into an executive producing deal. Pilots are in the works for two new shows, both with a hip-hop perspective. One will let fans borrow a star's entourage for a day, while the other follows the daily life of Run-D.M.C.'s Run. He also produced a cable series for HBO called *Bad Boys of Comedy*, featuring up-and-coming African American comics.

True to his "ghetto fabulous" credentials, Combs introduced his own line of luxury wheel rims for automobiles called Sean John Wheels, in March 1995. It was a fitting endeavor because Combs himself helped popularize a flashy lifestyle in which impressive cars are a key part.

Combs also announced that he would sell half of Bad Boy Entertainment to the Warner Music Group in 2005 for $30 million. What comes next for this self-described renaissance man? The answer might be, "What can't Diddy do?"

Combs has shown that hard work and good instincts can take people as far as they want to go. In the meantime, he's launched hundreds of careers, including those of his artists and the countless newcomers he has mentored. He has taken hip-hop into the stratosphere, making its performers as big as their predecessors in rock 'n' roll. Wherever he puts his Midas touch, the sky is the limit for Sean "Diddy" Combs.

TIMELINE

1970   Sean Combs is born in Harlem, New York City.

1973   Combs's father is killed in a drug-related shooting.

1982   Combs's mother moves the family to Mount Vernon, New York.

1990   Combs lands an internship at Uptown Records.

1991   Combs plays a major role in developing Jodeci, whose *Forever My Lady* sells 2 million copies; nine people die at a charity basketball game and rap concert organized by Combs and Heavy D.

1992   Combs encourages Andre Harrell to sign Mary J. Blige and helps produce her successful debut, *What's the 411?*

1993   Combs discovers and signs the Notorious B.I.G.; is fired from Uptown; and soon resurrects Bad Boy with $15 million from Arista Records.

1994   Bad Boy puts out a slew of successful records; Tupac Shakur is shot igniting the East Coast/West Coast beef.

1995   Combs starts Daddy's House Social Programs, Inc.

1996   Bad Boy releases 112's debut, *112*, and signs Black Rob and Ma$e. Tupac Shakur dies from a gunshot wound in Las Vegas; Combs releases his first solo single, "Can't Nobody Hold Me Down."

1997 The Notorious B.I.G. is killed by gunfire; Bad Boy releases his album *Life After Death*; Combs puts out "I'll Be Missing You," a tribute to Biggie; Combs launches Sean John and releases his solo debut, *No Way Out*.

1998 Combs is nominated for seven Grammy Awards, five American Music Awards, and five Soul Train Awards.

1999 Combs releases his second solo album, *Forever*; Combs is arrested after a shooting at Club New York in Manhattan.

2000 Combs is tried for the shooting at Club New York.

2001 Combs is declared not guilty on weapons possession and bribery charges arising out of the Club New York shooting; makes his film debut in *Made*; and has a supporting role in *Monster's Ball*.

2002 Combs stars in and produces *Making the Band 2* for MTV.

2004 Combs takes to the Broadway stage in *A Raisin in the Sun* and is named Menswear Designer of the Year by the Council of Fashion Designers of America.

2005 Combs signs a deal with MTV to put out several new shows; sells half of Bad Boy Entertainment for $30 million.

GLOSSARY

A and R "Artists and repertoire," the staff at a record company that scouts, signs, and grooms new talent.

benjamins Refers to hundred-dollar bills, which bear the image of Benjamin Franklin.

crossover Going from one genre of music to another, or straddling two different genres at once, such as pop and hip-hop, or hip-hop and R & B.

demo A sampler of an artist's work that he or she gives to others in hopes of securing a record deal.

gangsta rap Hard-core hip-hop that tells explicit tales of criminal lifestyle.

ghetto fabulous Refers to displays of wealth (sometimes excessive) by those raised in the inner city.

hard-core Often referring to hip-hop lyrics or music that describe the harsh reality of the streets, usually with harsh language and depictions of violence and sex.

hip-hop soul A blend of hip-hop beats and attitude with traditional R & B vocals.

new jack swing A danceable, radio-friendly genre of hip-hop popular in the late 1980s and early 1990s.

sellout An underground or lesser-known artist who betrays his or her origins to sell more records.

FOR MORE INFORMATION

Bad Boy Entertainment, Inc.
8-10 West 19th Street, 9th Floor
New York, NY 10011

Blue Flame Marketing and Advertising
1440 Broadway, 14th Floor
New York, NY 10018
(212) 381-2025

Daddy's House Social Programs, Inc.
P.O. Box 332
New York, NY 10018
(877) 786-3433

Sean John Clothing Company
525 Seventh Avenue
New York, NY 10018
(212) 869-6422

Due to the changing nature of Internet links, the Rosen Publishing Group, Inc., has developed an online list of Web sites related to the subject of this book. This site is updated regularly. Please use this link to access the list:

http://www.rosenlinks.com/lhhb/seco

FOR FURTHER READING

Green, Jared. *Rap and Hip Hop* (Examining Pop Culture). San Diego, CA: Greenhaven Press, 2003.

Haskins, Jim. *One Nation Under a Groove: Rap Music and Its Roots.* New York, NY: Jump at the Sun/Hyperion Books for Children, 2000.

Lommel, Cookie. *The History of Rap Music* (African American Achievers). Northborough, MA: Chelsea House Publications, 2001.

Torres, John. *P-Diddy* (Blue Banner Biographies). Hockessin, DE: Mitchell Lane Publishers, 2004.

BIBLIOGRAPHY

Cable, Andrew. *A Family Affair: The Unauthorized Sean "Puffy" Combs Story.* New York, NY: Ballantine Books, 1998.

Ro, Ronin. *Bad Boy: The Influence of Sean "Puffy" Combs on the Music Industry.* New York, NY: Pocket Books, 2001.

Thipgen, David E. "Streetwise, Boardroom Savvy, He Is the Music's Ambassador of Cool." *Time*, February 8, 1999.

INDEX

About the Author

Philip Wolny grew up in Queens, New York, enjoying the music of Run-D.M.C., LL Cool J, Slick Rick, and Ice-T at backyard barbecues. He currently resides in Los Angeles, California, where he is a writer and editor.

Photo Credits

Cover, pp. © 13, 27, Getty Images, Inc.; p. 1 © Mike Blake/Reuters/ Corbis; pp. 8, 17 © Reuters/Corbis; p. 10 © Mark Savage/Corbis; p. 15 © Mitchell Gerber/Corbis; p. 21 © The Everett Collection; p. 22 © Trapper Frank/Corbis Sygma; pp. 25, 26, 29, 33, 36, 41 © AP/Wide World Photos; p. 35 © Tricia Meadows/Globe Photos, Inc.; p. 39 © Michael Kim/Corbis.

Designer: Thomas Forget; Editor: Wayne Anderson